LIFE

Joys and Challenges

Happy Reading
Sr. Ethel Devlin

Ethel M. Devlin, s.e.j.

Order this book online at www.trafford.com
or email orders@trafford.com

Most Trafford titles are also available at major online book retailers.

© Copyright 2011 Ethel M. Devlin, s.e.j.

All rights reserved. No part of this publication may be reproduced, stored in a retrieval system, or transmitted, in any form or by any means, electronic, mechanical, photocopying, recording, or otherwise, without the written prior permission of the author.

Printed in the United States of America.

ISBN: 978-1-4269-6412-1 (sc)
ISBN: 978-1-4269-6413-8 (e)

Trafford rev. 04/12/2011

 www.trafford.com

North America & international
toll-free: 1 888 232 4444 (USA & Canada)
phone: 250 383 6864 ♦ fax: 812 355 4082

Dedication

To Mom and Dad and all their descendants.
May they grow in Love and Joy!

Acknowledgements

To relatives and friends who inspired me to write this book:

The Sisters of the Child Jesus, Elder Michael Harris, Gitxsan Nation, Omer Devlin, Gerry and Tammie Hamel, Frances Crawford, the Students and Staff of the Cariboo Residential School, 1966-1982, Larry Hamel, Lorne Hansen, Carmie Devlin, without whose expertise "Life: Joys and Challenges" would not have been completed.

Thank you all!

Contents

THE PASTURE	1
SQUIRRELS IN THE ATTIC?	5
OF BOYS AND DOGS	11
HIDDEN TREASURE	15
A TIME TO HEAL	19
BUCKIE	23
ALL RIGHT!	28
SWEAT BATHING	34
PREPARING FOR A VISION QUEST	38

THE PASTURE

My parents sold our farm in Vawn, Saskatchewan, in 1944. Extremely poor crops, drought, wind and dust conspired against our stay; we had to leave or perish.

I loved the old farm despite its many hardships; I dreaded leaving. New owners would take over in a week, leaving little time to say goodbye to good friends and relatives, to visit once again the places and animals I loved. I felt compelled to find some small treasure to take as a keepsake.

Dressed in faded blue jeans, an old red shirt and yellow-banded straw hat, I headed for the pasture, the place I had spent many happy hours.

There was no gate nearby so I got down on hands and knees to gingerly crawl under the three stranded barbed wire fence. As I emerged on the other side, two saucy prairie dogs stood perfectly upright, one emitting a low whistle, before both scampered into their holes. Could they be making fun of me or laughing at my expense? *Never mind their antics,* I thought.

A gorgeous mountain bluebird sat on a fence post near the well-worn trail I followed. The bluebird greeted the rising sun with its sweet song but usually remained silent and busy for the remainder of the day. I prayed its kind would flourish and bring peace and elation to all who saw it.

The slough in the middle of the pasture exuded a scent of decaying vegetation. It served as a watering hole for the farm animals and wild life. It also provided my family with water for the garden. A pair of mallard ducks swimming side by side, quacked to one another, then, suddenly dived straight down to feed from the bottom of the slough. I admired the way they were able to keep heads and breasts under water before coming up with a beak of goodies to relish.

Beyond the water, on a low rise our reddish brown Jersey, Strawberry, lay among the small trees and contentedly chewed her cud. The leaves of the nearby trees cast dancing patterns of shade upon her. The cow mooed softly as I approached to pat her head. Strawberry gave the creamiest milk of our seven cows.

She was the source of a small but steady income since we sold the butter made from the cream.

Strawberry turned her head towards a bird flying lopsided at the edge of the rise. *Something is wrong with that poor bird,* I thought, then laughed as I realized it was a protective gesture, feigning a broken wing to lure me away from her nest of eggs or young.

"You funny bird," I said aloud, yet felt grateful nature was so well equipped to give special traits, such as coloration, speed, size, strength or showmanship to creatures such as the killdeer.

At the head of the slough, saskatoon bushes thrived in a rough, circular space where wild flowers and catrinas grew in the tall grass. A couple of large stones served as seats. I loved to stop in this quiet spot, sit on one of the stones and allow my senses to experience the cool scented air, the peace and serenity of this simple retreat. On this day, I was reluctant to leave but a voice within assured me it was all part of the Mighty Plan.

Our dog, Sailor, barked, a call to return to the house, then I saw him chasing a gopher. Near me, an extended series of clear flutelike notes filled the air. The singer was a jaunty little brown fellow with a bright yellow vest emblazoned with a remarkably large black vee on his chest. He was a meadowlark singing a wonderful tune, no other bird could imitate. This bird is surely the Prince of the Prairies.

Peanut, our funny white horse, raised his head as the meadowlark sang. When Peanut is hitched to a buggy, the driver and friends must refrain from speaking words ending in "o" because the horse would immediately stop in the middle of the road. His ears seemed always perked to hear "whoa".

I returned home without a tangible keepsake but my time searching was not lost. Each place and creature of nature had imprinted itself indelibly on my soul. They awaken when I'm reminded of my years on the farm in Saskatchewan. I love those memories!

SQUIRRELS IN THE ATTIC?

A rowdy, mad rush very like stampeding animals bursts forth in the attic over my head. *What can it be? Is it my imagination?*

Oh, no! There it is again. Shaking, I make a dive for the telephone and call my landlord neighbor, Wilfred. He arrives in a minute.

"What's eating you?" he shouts entering the house. Another wild scrambling accompanied by eerie cries, answers Wilfred's question and a wide grin covers his face.

"Squirrels, you've got squirrels in your attic," then after a pause, "but don't worry, Sagar and I will get rid of them."

Get rid of them? All I want is that they get them out. I hope they won't get hurt in the process.

Wilfred calls his 8 year-old grandson. He comes in beaming from ear to ear at the thought of chasing squirrels.

Sagar, like his grandfather, sees the bright side of every hurdle. His sparkling blue eyes reflect his positive attitude and energetic drive while his red hair says, "Don't push me."

Sagar loves his grandfather and is always ready to run an errand for him or chase a squirrel.

"Come on, Sagar, let's take a look in the attic." Man and boy airily climb the narrow stairway leading the attic. All seems quiet.

"You go that way and check the space where the roof meets the wall and floor. You may find a nest. Mother squirrels like a cozy nest in a warm dry attic. When their babies are born the mother keeps them hidden for a while. I'll look along this wall and we'll meet over there," instructs Wilfred as he points to the middle of the wall opposite where they stand.

Sagar gets down on his knees and runs his hand lightly along the angle made by roof and floor. He feels something unusual but it's only a small rubber ball covered with dust and lint. As he nears the first corner, Sagar notices bits of old burlap, pieces of string, soiled cotton batting and other material he does not recognize, heaped together in a slight dip in the wall. *This is strange,* he thinks as he gingerly feels the softness under his hand. Suddenly, he realizes he found a nest.

Excited now, Sagar calls, "Grandpa, come see, I think I found a nest."

Wilford bends to examine the funny pile of stuff.

"It is a nest, Sagar," Grandpa assures him. "You are quick at finding things."

"Let's finish our search, before we go out to find how those squirrels got in here."

No other nests are found, so the two go outside and begin another search under the edge of the eaves. There must be a hole gnawed by the critters to get inside!

Grandfather goes to get the 10 foot ladder while Sagar walks slowly around the house with his eyes fixed under the eaves.

Near the corner of the house, close to the place Sagar found the nest, he now espies a black spot and wonders, *Can that be a hole?* At that moment a squirrel comes around the corner and disappears into the hole.

"Grandpa, a squirrel just ran into the house over here," Sagar says pointing to the hole.

"You have the sharp eyes of an eagle," Granddad proudly tells Sagar. "Come over to the shop, we'll make a door for that hole."

"It will have to be a one way door, Grandpa, but how will we make it?"

Sagar's face shows concern, something is bothering him.

"What is it Sagar? Where is that twinkle in your eye? Did I say something wrong?" enquires Grandpa.

"It's the squirrels, Grandpa. Will something bad happen to them?"

"Oh, no! You see, they'll be more happy than they are now. We'll give them all the freedom they want. Now, let's get at that one way door."

Wilfred got a strip of hardware cloth. "Watch as I turn up a lip along one side of this. You can help me but be careful not to get poked or scratched. Work from the underside, and roll the edge away from you. Come on out and we'll nail the straight edge around the hole, with the curved edge outside, away from the center. Now the squirrels can leave the attic without getting hurt but they cannot get back in.

"I'm glad they can't get caught in anything," observes Sagar, "but where will the squirrels go now?"

"Come with me, Sagar," answered Grandpa walking toward a grove of spruce trees growing in a field a couple of blocks away. Sagar is surprised and happy to see the trees.

"Grandpa, do you think the squirrels will come here if we drop peanuts along the way as a trail for them to follow?"

As the two approached Grandpa's house on the way back from the farm, Grandpa stated, "I bought peanuts to do just as you mentioned. If you want to make a trail, I'll go along and carry the bag."

They placed the balance of peanuts under the trees and hurried back to my house. On the way back they met several squirrels busy filling their cheeks.

Sagar laughed to see the squirrels' fat cheeks. "Race you back, Grandpa," he calls, making a dash.

While the two men are finishing up outside, I'm preparing a light snack in the kitchen. This is an awesome day for Sagar. As he comes into the kitchen followed by his grandfather, I notice the gleam of accomplishment on his face. It lights up even more as he sees the red, yellow and green balloons, the dish of candy on the counter for after the snack, and the pair of red gloves by his glass of milk.

"Thank you, Jenny," he says as he gives me a hug.

"Thank you both. You are such kind neighbors."

To this day I have not heard any more noise from the attic.

OF BOYS AND DOGS

Are German Shepherds able to be both watchdogs and family pets?

You tell me!

Czar and Zena, two noble, intelligent Alsatian dogs, stood over my neighbor's property; one male, the other female. Two young boys approached the dogs. The five year old, Sagar, hugged the female; she turned and licked his face and hands. The 11 year old, Chyle, called out to Czar who turned and nuzzled his young master. Amicably the boys and dogs raced toward the house and disappeared down the basement stairs.

Czar, the older dog, was a puppy when Gerry and Tammie welcomed their first child, a gentle little fellow, Chyle. The boy and the pup grew up together – Chyle, playful and fun loving; Czar, serious and protective. When the little tyke crawled away, Czar got his teeth in Chyle's diaper and pulled him back within his travelling limits.

Chyle referred to Czar as "my best buddy" and "a work dog, more a business dog". Czar was always on the alert for strangers whom he regarded with suspicion.

"He's awsome!" Chyle would say.

Czar learned to sit, heel, come, drop the leash, and sit close to the trainer's right leg, in obedience school. Chyle, at about eight years, became Czar's walker.

Czar started his work at seven in the morning. He went around the yard and closely examined every object lying around the yard, every car, every garage, shed, canopy or structure no matter how simple or complex they happened to be. If anyone came near the fence, Czar was right there barking or growling, if necessary, to make them move on.

Zena joined the family as a week old pup; Sagar was three at the time. Zena nipped and scratched everyone including Sagar, who was undaunted by her rough play. She ran to the sandbox as Sagar tried making roads and bridges but soon the constructions were demolished and sand flew in every direction. When

Sagar tried to wrestle Zena, she bit and clawed at him in self-defense but her behavior did not faze Sagar.

As Zena grew she followed Czar around the yard to learn when to bark and how often a watchdog should make the rounds. Zena's bark differed from Czar's bark; hers was higher, louder and more insistent; his was deeper with more authority. When Zena got too loud and busy with what did not concern her, Czar had a way of nudging her to be quiet.

The dogs differed in physical appearance: Czar had short fur and seemed always groomed. He was mostly black with generous portions of chocolate brown along the neck, legs, and below the ears. Zena was larger than Czar. She had a bushy tail, was mostly black with soft fur accented by long, pale tan gossamer strands of hair falling along her neckline, legs and paws. Her nose was pitch black like her shiny eyes. The black of her face made her appear full of mischief.

Zena did not go to obedience school but the family wanted her to be a guard dog. To this end Chyle tried to walk Zena after school. She would stand on her hind legs, place her front legs around Chyle, and squeeze him to stop him from clipping the leash to her collar. When he had her leashed, she barked at everyone they met.

"That one is not docile," observed a lady they encountered one day. For some time Zena's behavior embarrassed Chyle but at the last he was able to control her and lead her. In fact, Zena acquired a minimum amount of composure and dignity.

Neither dog tolerated other animals. A raccoon descended from his perch on a garage then came down into their yard.

In a flash Zena had the critter's head; Czar had the other end. The boys' grandfather called the dogs off. The raccoon crawled up a tree, Zena's face was badly scratched but Czar escaped unscathed.

In unison the boys exclaimed,

"Cool!"

To answer my question, I think dogs can be good watchdogs <u>and</u> great family pets. What do you think?

HIDDEN TREASURE

"Chilliwack's Water Supply"

Chilliwack, British Columbia, home of the Bruins, tourist attraction and playground for all ages, is noted for its mild climate, fertile soil, and comfortable location.

Encircled by mountains, it developed in the crisscrossing of three major rivers, the Fraser, the Chilliwack, and the Vedder. Several creeks, the Luckakuck, the Coqualeetza, the Atchelitz, to name a few, once teemed with fish. In the mid 1800's, time of the first white settlers in the valley, Indian canoes gracefully glided over the waterways in search of food, to visit friends or to enjoy Mother Nature. The Stó:lō Nation came to the area between 11,000 and 5,500 B.C., at the time the ice sheet melted enough to allow people to be self-sufficient.

Ancient history interprets geographical changes through legends handed down since time immemorial. The First Nation, Stó:lō, used a source of pure water for drinking, cooking, bathing and cleaning.

The Sardis-Vedder Aquifer is Chilliwack's most awesome feature and its greatest potential problem. The eight square kilometer aquifer supplies the 60,000 residents of Chilliwack and surrounding area with 25,000,000 million litres of water each day. No chemicals are added to the water. Its high quality meets the Canadian federal guidelines.

Webster's dictionary defines aquifer as a composite of aqua and fer. Aqua means water; fer means bearer. Aquifer means bearer of water.

The Sardis-Vedder Aquifer is a natural underground reservoir, a large pocket of water formed by the Chilliwack River where it exits the Cascade Mountains. The aquifer is a fan-shaped alluvial deposit of permeable rock: permeable because the connecting pores allow water to move freely through them.

As the water, confined in the rock, is used up, it is replaced by groundwater from the Vedder River, from local rain or melting snow, and from surface runoff. These waters percolate into the aquifer but are not in direct contact with it. Surface water will carry contaminants through the porous layer of gravel and soil, in places one meter deep, above the aquifer.

Contaminated water can cause serious illness and even death to those who drink it. Contaminants come from chemicals left on the ground, poisons, sewage from broken pipes or drains, garbage dumps, manure, pesticides, and harmful bacterial growth in places having improper drainage or drainage into one of the waterways. Any impurity left on the ground will be carried, by water, into the soil by force of gravity. To ensure good quality, groundwater from the Sardis-Vedder Aquifer is analyzed from eight sites, every two months.

Several wells have been drilled into the aquifer, the first in 1964, by the Department of National Defense, at the army base. In addition to the wells in the city, over one hundred private wells have been drilled to serve industries, farms, and homes in outlying areas.

The provincial government is currently working on drinking water standards for British Columbia. The City of Chilliwack supports standards affecting everyone in the province. The City is asking residents outside city limits, to take preventive measures to safeguard their wells from contamination. Some steps, for ensuring good quality water, are as follows:

1. Hire a certified contractor to build a well, and mark its exact position.
2. Keep storage sheds and bins a safe distance from the well.
3. Be sure the top of the well is, at least, one foot above flood level, and surrounding ground slopes away from the well.
4. Make sure the well is capped and sealed.
5. Never use abandoned wells as places for hazardous materials; rather, cap and grout them.
6. Check wells regularly for cracks, rusting, damaged casing, missing caps and cracked surface seals.
7. Have septic system inspected regularly.

People living in Chilliwack are proud of their city and grateful for their hidden treasure. In 1997 and 1999, last year of the contest, the City received an award from the Canadian Water Resource Association for having best drinking water in Canada. In 1998, Chilliwack received second place award.

A TIME TO HEAL

Carmen Johnstone recalled the day at age four, when she awoke in so much pain she could not get out of bed. She had contracted polio which left her first crippled in one leg. Then Pyrthes' Hip settled into her other side. Now both legs refused to carry her.

C.C. and Grace Johnstone, directed by their doctor, took their only child to the Queen Alexandria Solarium for crippled children, on Vancouver Island. They traveled first by car to Vancouver Harbor, by Blackball ferry to Victoria Harbor, finally by car to Cobble Hill.

Carmen's eyes brightened and opened wide at the sight of so many little children at her new home. She fretted as a nurse took her to a bed in a dorm where she would spend the first part of her healing.

Carmen was given exercises to strengthen her shoulders and arms in preparation for using a shoulder harness and a pair of crutches. Time spent exercising was painful and felt endless. Three weeks into her stay, Carmen acquired her first crutches and paten. This marked the beginning of a little more independence even if she could only stand. Slowly, she became more adept and balanced in her movements, able to navigate among the other small patients.

She reached a milestone the first time she had enough balance to carry a drink of water to her special friend, Tinkabell. After that incident, Carmen often carried a toy or water to other patients needing attention.

The Johnstone's often sent Maple Buds to be shared by the children and staff. One day, Carmen mysteriously disappeared. No one noticed where she went after breakfast. Her absence was obvious during exercise period.

"Didn't anyone notice where Carmen went?" asked the nurse, looking from one little face to the next. At the end of the last row of children, the nurse saw a tiny boy pointing his index finger toward the candy cupboard. The nurse followed the lead and just out of sight stood four-year-old Miss Johnstone with chocolate smeared around her mouth and chin while rivulets of the brown stuff ran down the front of her pinafore.

"Good chocolate," beamed the child as she looked up at the adult. The nurse now led Carmen to the washroom, cleaned her up, then followed her to the exercise room. The staff had a great chuckle that evening as they relaxed over a cup of tea before making preparations for the following day and retiring for the night.

Carmen missed her Mom and Dad. She was too young to understand why they were unable to come more often. She was prone to having bouts of severe earaches, high fever and tonsillitis. The latter got so bad she was admitted to the Victoria Hospital for an operation. Visitors were not permitted at the hospital, it was thought patients would get worse if distracted by anyone. Back at the solarium after her operation, Carmen was confined to her bed until able to navigate her crutches again.

Miss Andrews, Carmen's favorite nurse, wrote monthly letters to the Johnstone's. She praised Carmen's usual good disposition, and her sweet captivating, loving ways which made her the most popular kiddie in the solarium. Mrs. Johnstone treasured the pile of letters she kept to give later to her daughter.

Carmen's good nature and progress won for her the title "Cover Girl" for the annual booklet prepared for the public of British Columbia. The booklet presented an update of the work done for crippled children at the solarium and requested financial support to ensure the good work continued.

In October, 1944, Carmen was discharged from the Solarium and walked away on her crutches with confidence. The sights she saw and life's lessons she learned at a young age never left her. The tiny seed of kindness, she brought from home to the Solarium, sprouted during the fifteen months of her stay and continued to grow and flourish after her discharge.

Today, Carmen is one of the nine directors of a Community Foundation, a perpetual trust fund with six million dollars capital. All investment proceeds from the trust are yearly distributed to community charitable organizations and post secondary students.

BUCKIE

A tired, frightened puppy crawled into the yard where Justin aged "6" and Sarah "4" lived. He was splashed with mud, and hardly recognizable as a wavy haired Cocker Spaniel. Sara was afraid of the small tan colored dog but her brother, Justin, loved it right away. Justin ran into the house to get milk for the dog and a doggy biscuit for Sarah to give him.

The puppy gulped down the milk and biscuit then crawled under a nearby azalea bush. Justin coaxed him to come out from his uncomfortable shelter but the pup crawled backward to hide from view.

Grandmother lived across the street from her grandchildren, Justin and Sarah. Granny, as the children called her, saw the little dog wiggle under the white gate. Now she watched through the window to see what would happen next.

Granny saw Justin and Sarah push the wading pool to the hose. Justin turned on the hose and half filled the little pool. Both children coaxed the dog to go into the water but the dog would not budge.

They want to give the dog a bath but they have no shampoo, no towel, thought Granny. *Nor can they get him to come out from that bush.*

This will help, thought Granny, as she picked up a dog dish filled with Kibbles and Bits. *A bottle of shampoo and a towel will be all they need,* she thought.

The children thanked Granny. They took the food to the bush calling, "Here puppy," as they crouched down and pushed it close to him. While the puppy ate hungrily, Justin placed his hand on it and gradually pulled the dog to himself. It relaxed.

Now Justin brought the dog to the edge of the pool. The dog jumped into the pool. Sarah put shampoo on the dog. Both children rubbed it on his back, head, ears, legs and tail. Soon the pup looked like a ball of snow but the suds disappeared as soon as the dog was rinsed off. The children laughed and clapped for the little dog.

The dog jumped from the pool in a flash, gave himself a brisk shake and sent sprinkles of water on Granny and the children. Justin and Sarah dried him off a little more. They now emptied the wading pool and stood it against the garage.

Now they all took 'time out' to sit in the sun. The humans were happy but the little animal seemed sad. He did not play nor did he go sniffing around.

"Something is the matter with that dog," said Justin.

Ray and Linda, the children's parents, came out from the house just as the discussion about the dog was going on. They too, wondered why the puppy seemed so quiet.

Granny got up from the box on which she sat. She tottered and had to sit down again.

"I'm having a dizzy spell. Would you take me to the clinic, Ray?" Ray backed the car from the garage and helped Granny into it.

A doctor took Granny's pulse and ordered her to go straight to the hospital. Granny was admitted and given a bed right away. Ray promised he'd bring the family over the next afternoon.

The next day the family and the little dog went to visit Granny. She felt much better but the doctor said they would keep her under observation for at least a week.

As the family prepared to leave the hospital, a long chaise pushed by an attendant approached.

A young, redheaded child of 5 or 6 years, half sat, leaning on a pillow. His little face was pale and thin and his eyes were partly closed.

All of a sudden, the puppy gave a yap, jumped upon the chaise and licked the little boy's face.

"Buckie," cried the child, "where were you?"
"I missed you so much," he said as he threw his arms around the dog.

"Is he your dog?" inquired Justin.

"Yes," answered the boy.

"Someone took him outside, but did not bring him back!"

"My name's Tim, what is yours?"

"I'm Justin and this is my sister, Sarah. We were so happy your dog came to our house. He was not happy and we couldn't understand why. Now, its plain to see, he belongs to you and he's happy to have found you."

Buckie was not allowed to remain in the hospital every day, but Justin and Sarah took him along each time they visited Tim. Tim always looked forward to seeing his little dog and his new friends. He soon got stronger and color came back into his face.

One day Granny left her hospital bed and came to meet her grandchildren. They gathered in a small room, a kind nurse had shown them.

As soon as all were seated, Tim gathered Buckie in his arms, saying "Buckie, you are the best dog. You found new friends for me. Thank you, Sarah, thank you, Justin and Granny. I will come to visit you after the doctor lets me go home. That time is coming soon."

So it happened!

ALL RIGHT!

Seth loved his second year of drumming for the Laker School band in Hopeful. Almost 15 now, he set a daily routine for himself to offset after school band practice.

He was up at 6 each morning, reviewed social study and English facts, took out the garbage, swept the porch, showered and was ready to join the family for breakfast at 7. Sticking to a demanding routine was difficult, but Seth was determined not to get behind in his schoolwork.

Monday to Wednesday is easy, he thought, *but I have to psyche myself up for Friday and Thursday. I'd hate to backslide in school. It would be hard to claw my way up again.*

Dan and Mary, Seth's parents, noticed their son looked tired. They asked him not to be so hard on himself. They worried that he needed more sleep, yet, they didn't want to be over-controlling. They knew he was struggling to gain independence. They decided to wait and hope.

Seth, on his way to school, was busy mulling over plans for the week. He put his skateboard down on the bicycle lane and propelled himself at a good clip down the slight incline toward the school. As he crossed Third Street, he caught sight of a girl walking beside a boy in a wheelchair. Seth stopped and waited for the pair.

"Hello," he said, "I'm Seth, I go to Laker School. You're new around here, aren't you?"

The boy answered for both. "I'm Pete, and this is my twin, Tiffany, Tiff for short". Pete, with half-closed, accusing eyes, turned his face away. His hostile looks and curt answer puzzled Seth.

Could it be the wheelchair? wondered Seth. *His arms and hands seem strong and muscular. He must have pumped iron in a rehab situation. I wonder....* Seth cut short his thought to ask, "What is your favorite subject, Pete?"

For a long moment, the sulky youth made no reply, then he blurted out, "I'm average in school subjects. I was good in basketball until a car accident put me in this," nodding down at the wheelchair. "Doctors don't think I'll walk again, neither do I," he added, staring sullenly at the distant mountains.

Tiff turned toward her brother. "Don't worry, Pete. Things will change. We've been here only a couple of weeks. Dad will find work and you'll get more therapy. Come on! We'd better not be late first day at school." The trio went on in silence.

Seth's forehead creased in concern. *Pete has a problem,* he thought. *How could I help him? I get the impression he doesn't like it here. Pete is testy. I should talk to them,* he decided, downing the last of his ham sandwich. He looked around the cafeteria and spied the twins sitting together on the fringe of the student diners, their backs to the crowd. Seeing them isolated, Seth was more determined than ever to help them feel accepted at school.

On the way home after band practice, Seth wondered what he would do about Pete and Tiff. He picked up the newspaper at the door and sat on the steps to check the sports page. A report on a soccer game played at Pyke, 15 miles away, got his attention. He read "The players were all in wheelchairs, three of them from Hopeful." Seth sprang up. *Town Hall will know how to contact athletes groups. I'll give them a call,* he thought.

Seth dialed the number. A message came on. "You have reached Town Hall. Our offices are open from 8:30 a.m. to 4:30 p.m., Monday to Friday. Please consult the blue pages of your local phone book for further information. Thank you. Click." Seth replaced the receiver. There wouldn't be time in the morning. He had an hour to go through the material at the library.

Entering, he headed for the books on sports. The first book, PEOPLE WITH DISABILITIES, was too general; those following were thick and detailed. There wasn't time to search. As Seth turned to leave, a display rack at the end of the sports books, caught his eye. A number of brochures targeted various wheelchair sports. A big grin lit Seth's face as he picked out three pamphlets. There were no bar codes on the material, so, no need to check at the desk. He walked back home with lighter steps.

Seth caught up with Tiff and Pete just as they were leaving the school. Pete stopped abruptly, whipped his chair around, attempting to avoid Seth. Seth kept his cool as he said, "You are interested in basketball. Take a moment to look at these." He offered the brochures to Pete who yanked them from his hand.

Tiff, embarrassed by her brother's attitude, tried to calm his hostility by speaking quietly, "Pete, it won't hurt to look at those. Come over to the cement block by the trees."

The first handout was a colored triple-fold entitled *Bridging the Gap*, and read in part: "Bridging the Gap is a program presented by the B.C. Wheelchair Sports Association (BCWSA). Its aim is to help individuals become reintegrated into the community and regain their motivation, inspiration, independence and confidence."

The BCWSA offered weekly programs in power soccer, tennis, basketball, rugby, target sports, athletics and hockey.

As Pete read on, he started relaxing. The mountains of obstacles he had built began to crumble. At first, the pamphlets seemed useless and empty but when Pete raised his head and looked into Seth's eyes, the sullenness had gone. The self-pity, into which he wrapped himself, gave way to reality. Pete suddenly realized he was a strong, capable person who had permitted himself to be punished by his injury.

He picked up the brochure on which was printed a form for requesting program and membership information.

"Let's go home, Tiff. I have to speak to Mom and Dad right away. I understand now, others are far worse off than I. My wheelchair can open the door to many sports. I want to be part of a team."

Turning to Seth who looked rather stunned by this transformation, Pete held out his hand.

"You've been a real friend, Seth. It's taken me too long to realize it. You and Tiff have been awesome."

Seth was still standing by the cement block when Pete and Tiff waved goodbye. He picked up his pack-sack, shook his head in disbelief, then threw his arms into the air shouting, "All Right!"

SWEAT BATHING

The late Chief Dan George, Tsleil-Waut, beloved leader of the People of the Inlet, Burrard, actor and public speaker, often had his audience howling with merriment at his witty observations. Once, he opened his talk by comparing the First Nations' bathing habits with those of the white population. He said, "You Whites, rub and scrub yourselves to get clean but all you do is push the dirt deeper. We, Natives take sweat baths to force the grime and dirt out of the pores. We sweat it out!"

Sweat bathing is carried out in small shanty-like structures sequestered in a quiet wood near lake, or running water. Many of these tiny lodges are fabricated from sturdy saplings arranged dome-like and covered with tarps, hides or blankets and built on reservations. An overlap of blanket or tarp serves as an entrance through which one must bend low or crawl to enter.

A fire pit near the entrance, is used to heat stones, later carried into the structure to provide an abundance of steam when water is sprinkled upon them.

Native Canadians or First Nations, as they are called today, practice sweat bathing as a deeply religious exercise of prayer, healing and as an expression of unity and identification with tribal brothers and sisters as well as with plants, animals, or even inanimate objects like stone.

Native tribes stress harmony above all else. They perceive our planet as a blend of four elements, earth, water, fire and air. Balance among the four elements produces harmony and beauty.

The Great Creator Spirit gave the planet earth four directions, north, south, east and west, and to each direction assigned a race of people, red skinned, black skinned, yellow skinned and white skinned. The Great Spirit breathed life into all people and creatures and endowed them with gifts for all, to be shared by all.

The Great Spirit placed Mother Earth as guardian over creation, to oversee the elements, the seasons and productions of each.

First Nation people, the red race, have the greatest admiration, love, and respect for Mother Nature and for her legacy. They are daily grateful for her gifts and take from her, plants and animals according to their need, always careful not to destroy or damage her treasurers.

The Native sweat lodge is more than a bathing facility, more than a sauna. It is a Sacred Place. Participants express prayer in chanting, personal reflection, humble admission of faults, and in gracious forgiveness of one another.

On an appointed day for sweat bathing, small groups of men or women silently gather together on the path leading to the lodge. They prefer early morning hours or sundown to participate in the Sacred Rite because there is relative stillness at that time. In silence they walk toward the small lodge hidden in a grove of trees growing near the water. Each person is deep in thought. Images of ill feelings, spats or spurts of anger replace one another in their minds. Each person feels sad about what happened in the interval since the last month's sweat. They want forgiveness; they want to make amends.

Smoke from the fire pit fills the air with its distinctive odor as the fire pit attendant, poker in hand, moves each rock a little to give it the advantage of the fire. The rocks must be red hot before they are placed in a small hollow inside the lodge. They will be carried by shovel once the participants are inside.

Now the first person bends low to crawl under the tarp flap used as an entrance. The others follow and each finds a place to kneel or sit in the dim light coming from the open flap. The fire attendant places the hot rocks inside the lodge then leaves the lodge, closing the flap behind him. A soft plaintiff chant rises. Someone joins in the chant. Now prayers and petitions are heard. The leader of the group sprinkles water, brought in earlier, on the rocks, which hisses as a cloud of steam fills the tiny chamber. The temperature rises. Prayers and chanting become more intense. More water is splashed as for a second time hot rocks are deposited in the inside pit. The surge of prayers rises again.

After about half an hour of spiritual fervor, the group becomes quiet. It is time to return home. One by one they leave through the now open flap entrance. In single file they go towards the river and plunge into the ice cold water. Laughter and joyful cries replace the quiet pondering. In a flash the group is out of the water, toweled and dressed, ready to face another day, or for a good night's sleep. Steps are light and hurried, some making little gazelle like leaps into the air as they hurry toward home and family.

It is good to be alive!

PREPARING FOR A VISION QUEST

Danny, a 14 year old Gitxsan Nation Youth, lived with his Grandfather, chief of the Wolf Clan. Danny was tall, handsome, with athletic build and princely deportment. He usually wore an easy slow smile, which gradually lit up his face, but at times seemed preoccupied with deep thoughts. His gait was light but determined. He liked to fish for rainbow trout in the Skeena River running in front of Grandfather's house.

Danny and his little sister, Starlite, came to live with Grandpa Elijah and Granny Mary when their parents were taken from them. Gabriel and his wife Stella, were plunged into a creek where a bridge had been washed away. The tragedy occurred one dark, stormy night as they returned home from a meeting. Danny often thought of his parents and felt grateful his grandparents had taken him and his sister in and given them a good home.

The Gitxsan Nation, like many other First Nation's people, regarded themselves as part of nature, as one with all nature's creatures. Many Gitxsan communicated with the spirits of animals. Some of the members believed animals communicated messages, gave them powers and dispelled fears. The Natives were also affiliated with all things of nature, i.e., plants, stones, the sun, the moon, the sky, the clouds. All creation was referred to and respected as brothers or sisters.

Grandfather Elijah often spoke to Danny about the culture of the people, about the young men who went on a vision quest to learn from the Creator what was necessary to become the man he was meant to be. Danny thought about the words spoken by his Grandfather. Some of those words were mysterious and required a lot of thought.

One night, Danny had an extraordinary dream. He saw himself as a young man, high on a mountain, sitting in a circle marked out on the soil around him. Within the circle, facing Danny, sat the Great Creator Spirit. Danny begged the Creator to make him strong, to take away his fears and to help him walk on the straight, often hard, paths before him. Danny awakened at the moment the Great Creator was about to speak.

Was that a dream or did I really sit before the Creator, Danny asked himself over and over again. As he flicked on the light he realized he had been asleep in his bed. *I had a dream but what a wonderful dream! What does it mean?*

Danny sought out his Grandfather to tell him of his dream. *Perhaps Papa will know when I should go on a vision quest.*

Papa Elijah was attentive to every word Danny said. He did not interrupt his grandson. When the youth finished speaking, the elderly man gazed at him but said nothing. After a long silence Grandfather responded in a solemn voice.

"Son, a vision quest is a difficult journey into your own heart where you speak to the Great Creator Spirit to find answers to all puzzles and pain hidden there. You will know when the time is right for you to make that journey. Beginning today, I will guide you through the preparations necessary for this journey. I will teach you the beliefs, customs and lore of your ancestors, just as my Grandfather taught me when I was your age. You must be very strong, prepared to consume little food and ready to bear the discomfort of sleeping out in the forest. It dealt with the four directions, East, South, West, and North. Today we begin with the first lesson."

East symbolized, "spirit, prayer, salvation." The Great Creator Spirit was reached in prayer by facing East. The eagle, most majestic of all birds, was the symbol of prayer because it flew higher than any bird. The eagle flew close to the Great Creator and was considered Sacred to the people. East was represented by the color, red.

South represented "beginning, newness, purity." Babies and small children symbolized South, as does the coyote, as it skulks about playing tricks on others. The coyote's actions were irresponsible just as children who passed the day playing, eating and sleeping. The color, yellow represented South.

West, home of the winds, represented by the color, black. The winds were always busy. They pushed the clouds hither and yonder where needed. They blew trees, made them lose their leaves. West signified busy workmen who toiled all day at one or several occupations to earn a living for themselves and their families.

North, represented by old age, the end of their long days. The aged were thought to be in the winter of life. Activities slowed, memories of days long passed lingered on. The buffalo's life seemed endless, like that of the very old. White, punctuated the cold of winter and its colorless days of North.

Danny sat motionless before his Grandfather. Tears flooded his eyes as Papa Elijah portrayed, in words, the various phases of life. The youth thought of his parents whom he missed so much, and of his grandparents who would soon fade like a sunset.

Grandfather noted sadness on the face of his grandson and his own heart questioned why life dealt such harsh lessons. Elijah's features changed suddenly, as he turned a warm, smiling face and twinkling black eyes toward Danny.

"Grandson," he began, "The sun is calling us outside. Come on, we'll surprise Granny with a nice big rainbow trout."

Danny jumped up. A slow smile spread over his face as he ran to fetch Grandpa's buckskin jacket and his own fleece one. Danny loved fishing. He felt so mature with his grandfather who talked to him, man to man.

Joy crept across his face as he thought of the campfire the two would build together to cook the fish. The Gitxsan Nation usually used nets, rarely rod and reel for fishing. Grandfather loved to go out, maybe catch one or two fish. He kept a couple of rods and reels, just in case.

Shaded by a grove of willow, the elder and the youth released the bails on their spinning reels and cast their lures. Suddenly Danny felt a tug and prepared to reel in, but just as suddenly the line slacked.

Must be weeds, Danny thought as he reeled in to clear the lure and cast again. The lure flew over the water, Danny eyed the beautiful trout on Grandpa's line.

"Oh, Grandpa," he shouted, "you've got a big one." Grandfather smiled as he slowly reeled in. Before the big trout reached shore, Danny knew his line too, held a big one.

Grandpa gutted the fish before he handed it to Grandma. Her big smile was reward enough for Grandpa.

The two adults and two children finished their delicious evening meal just as the sun began to set. Danny helped with the cleanup then hurried to his room.

Grandpa is so wise, he thought, *I wonder what he'll tell me tomorrow.* With that wishful thought tickling his anticipation, Danny washed up, jumped into bed and was asleep before his head hit the pillow. The excitement of the day took all the wind from his sails.

Danny rose at dawn, quickly ate breakfast, then went out for a run along the river trail. The rest of the family was up and around when Danny returned so he went immediately to his Grandfather. As he entered the room, Danny saw a bundle of red flannel, a can of tobacco, a roll of black string, and a pair of scissors on a small table beside his Grandfather.

Intrigued, Danny searched his elder's face for answers.

"Sit down, Grandson. Today we'll decide what we must take along on a vision quest."

Danny's heart beat faster. He was unable to prevent his feet from skipping a little as he sat down.

Grandfather cut a three-inch square piece of red flannel and held it flat on his open left hand. One corner lay over his middle finger while the corner diagonally opposite pointed to his wrist. Grandpa now took a pinch of tobacco about the size of a dime, laid it in the center of the red square, and after gathering the fabric around the knob of tobacco, he tied it snuggly with an 18 inch string. Both ends of the string were left dangling.

"The tobacco," explained Grandfather, "is an offering of gratitude to the Great Spirit for His protection and guidance during the four day vision quest. I will help you prepare 28 of these offerings. The number 28 denotes the number of days it takes the moon to travel around the earth. You may choose to prepare many more, which you can tie together into one continuous string. Now, Danny, cut a red square of cloth, using that cardboard piece I made for a pattern."

As Danny started cutting the red piece, his Grandfather gathered a bit of tobacco, rolled it into a ball and placed it upon the square Danny now held in the flat of his hand. Danny tied it with a string as Papa had done. Now Danny's first task was completed and he sighed as he relaxed.

"Danny, I will be your mentor when you are ready for your vision quest. Don't be in a hurry to begin. Ask the Creator to give you wisdom, and trust you will know when the time is right for you."

"Thank you, Grandfather, I will remember all you have taught me. You are the best mentor Grandpa, in all the world!" Grandpa smiled and hugged his grandson.

Everything fell into place, just as Grandpa said they would. Danny went through the smooth and bumpy stages of his development. When 16 summers had gone, Danny felt something big was about to happen. One night, in a dream, his Grandfather who now lived with the Creator, came to the young man. He touched him gently saying, "Danny, the time has come for you to go on your vision quest. Don't be afraid, I'll be with you all the way."

So it happened.

Ideas for <u>Preparing for a Vision Quest</u> came from an interview with Michael Harris, an Elder from the Gitxsan Nation, Hazelton, British Columbia. Mr. Harris received much of his cultural education from Medicine People, Elders, Research Books and Ethnologists. Mr. Harris has experienced a number of vision quests and is considered an expert in that field.

BIBLIOGRAPHY

Blomfield, Kate, et al. <u>A Stó:lo-Coast Salish Historical Atlas.</u> Seattle: University of Washington Press, 2001.

Wells, Oliver N. <u>The Chilliwacks and Their Neighbors.</u> Vancouver: Talons, 1987.

Protecting the Sardis-Vedder Aquifer: A Well Owner's Guide: City of Chilliwack leaflet.

Protecting The Sardis-Vedder Aquifer: Drinking Water Quality Information: City of Chilliwack leaflet.

Waller, Roger M., Ground Water and the Rural Homeowner, Pamphlet, U.S. Geological Survey, 1982. http://ga.water.usgs.gov/edu/earthwaquifer.html. May 13, 2003